I love reading

Busy Trucks

by Monica Hughes

Consultant: Mitch Cronick

BEARPORT
PUBLISHING COMPANY, INC.
New York, New York

Credits

t=top, b=bottom, c=center, l=left, r=right, OFC=outside front cover
Alvey & Towers: 5, 6. Corbis: 14–15. Peterbilt: 7, 10–11, 23tl, 23bl.
Superstock: 4, 19, 21. ticktock photography: 9, 11t, 12, 13, 16, 17, 18, 20, 22b.

Library of Congress Cataloging-in-Publication Data

Hughes, Monica.

   Busy trucks / by Monica Hughes.

      p. cm. — (I love reading)

   Includes index.

   ISBN 1-59716-150-0 (library binding) — ISBN 1-59716-176-4 (pbk.)

   1. Trucks — Juvenile literature. I. Title. II. Series.

TL230.15.H84 2006

629.224 — dc22

2005030942

For more information, write to Bearport Publishing Company, Inc., 101 Fifth Avenue, Suite 6R, New York, New York 10003. Printed in the United States of America.

1 2 3 4 5 6 7 8 9 10

The I Love Reading series was originally developed by Tick Tock Media.

CONTENTS

Busy trucks

Trucks have a **cab** where the driver sits.

Trucks have wheels with thick tires.

Cab

Tire

CA58816

The truck driver can sleep in the cab at night.

Cab

Engines

Trucks have engines.

The engines help the trucks move.

On some trucks, the engine is under the cab.

Cab

Engine

This truck has a long **hood**.

The engine is under the hood.

Hood

Exhaust

Trucks have an exhaust.

The exhaust takes gases away from the engine.

Cab

Exhaust

Engine

License plate

Two-part trucks

Some trucks have two parts.

The front part is the tractor.

The back part is the **trailer**.

The tractor has a cab,
an engine, and wheels.

Tractor

Trailer

Carrying cars

Some trucks can carry cars.

The cars are put on a trailer that hooks onto the tractor.

Trailer

Tractor

N827 CWP

VOLVO
FL10
INTERCOOLER

K135 ABW

13

Road trains

Road trains are very long trucks.

They have two or three trailers.

Trailers

Garbage trucks

A garbage truck takes away trash.

The trash is put into the
back of the truck.

Then the trash is crushed.

The crushed trash is unloaded at a **dump**.

Tankers

Tankers are trucks that have tanks in the back.

The tanks carry liquids or gases.

The liquid may be milk, oil, or gasoline.

Cab

Tank

This truck has two tanks.

Cement mixers

Cement mixers carry cement, sand, and **gravel** to make **concrete**.

These trucks have a big drum that turns around and around.

Drum

The drum mixes the concrete as it spins.

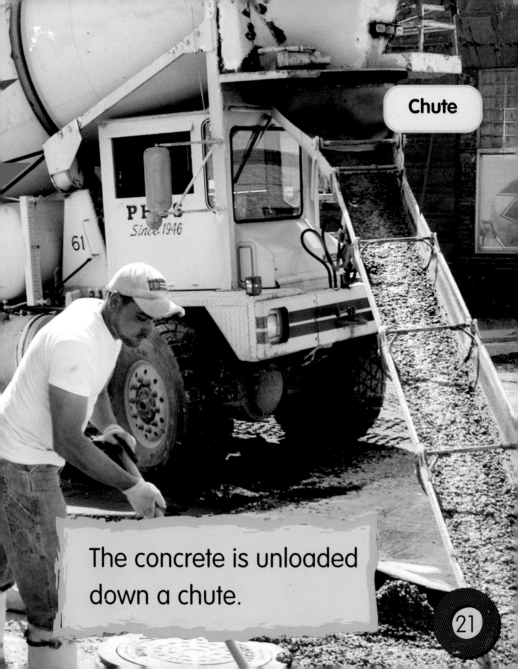

Chute

The concrete is unloaded down a chute.

Glossary

cab (KAB)
the place where
the truck driver sits

concrete (kon-KREET)
a mixture of sand, water,
cement, and gravel used
in construction

dump (DUHMP)
a place where
garbage is left

gravel (GRAV-uhl) small, crushed stones

hood (HUD) the front part of a truck

trailer (TRAYL-ur) the back part of a truck that carries things

Index

Learn More

Dussling, Jennifer. *Construction Trucks.* New York: Grosset & Dunlap (1998).

Relf, Patricia. *Tonka Big Book of Trucks.* New York: Scholastic (1996).

www.ci.seattle.wa.us/transportation/roadrunner/monstertrucks.htm

www.kenkenkikki.jp/zukan/e_dump_h00.html